Once Upon A Dream

Creative Voices

Edited By Allie Jones

First published in Great Britain in 2017 by:

Young Writers Est. 1991

Young Writers
Coltsfoot Drive
Peterborough
PE2 9BF
Telephone: 01733 890066
Website: www.youngwriters.co.uk

All Rights Reserved
Book Design by Ashley Janson
© Copyright Contributors 2017
SB ISBN 978-1-78820-978-6
Printed and bound in the UK by BookPrintingUK
Website: www.bookprintinguk.com
YB0316E

FOREWORD

Welcome to 'Once Upon A Dream - Creative Voices'.

For our 'Once Upon A Dream' competition, we invited primary school pupils to delve within their deepest imaginations and create poetry inspired by dreams. They were not limited to the dreams they experience during their sleep, they were free to explore and describe their dreams and aspirations for the future, what could inspire a dream, and also the darker side of dreams... the nightmare!

The topic proved to be hugely popular, with children dreaming up the cleverest, craziest and, sometimes, creepiest of poems! The entries we received showcase the writing talent and inspired imaginations of today's budding young writers.

Congratulations to Pippa Cudmore, who has been selected as the best poet in this anthology, hopefully this is a dream come true! Also a big well done to everyone whose work is included within these pages, I hope seeing it published help you continue living your writing dreams!

Allie Jones

CONTENTS

Winner:

Pippa Cudmore (10) - Gotherington Primary School, Cheltenham ... 1

Independent Entries

Megan Sarfas (11)	3
Mia Cleave (10)	4
Lily May Elizabeth Ormerod (9)	5
Hannah Jayne Bennett (10)	6
Grace Eve Bennett (10)	7
Rio Williams (9)	8

Aberdare Town CW Primary School, Aberdare

Abbey Amelia Broome (9)	9
Nerys Stocks (9)	10
Corey James Hansford (9)	11
Ffion Harris Stark (8)	12
Lucas Jesse Burford (9)	13
Morgan Matthews (8)	14
Carys Jones (9)	15
Kaitlyn Butterfill (8)	16
Hudson Blake Griffiths (9)	17
Emmie Sayce-Edwards (8)	18
Sophie Harries (8)	19
Jake Berry (8)	20
Morgan Evans (8)	21
Anna-Louise Grafham (9)	22
Ewan Milton (8)	23
Owen Lynam (8)	24
Kieran Rodda (8)	25
Tylor Sweet (8)	26
Madison Eve Shellard (8)	27
Kian Meyrick (8)	28
Owen North (8)	29
Ethan Carey (8)	30

Archbishop Rowan Williams (VA) CIW Primary School, Caldicot

Jacob Lee (10)	31
Arwen Skinner (10)	32
Kieran Howells (11)	34
Erin Beasley (10)	36
Charley Rockliffe-Fidler (10)	38
Iwan James Hall (10)	40
Lucy Nicholson (10)	41
Nia Davies (10)	42
Harvey Lewis Heaven (10)	44
Xavi-Mai Taylor (11)	45
Archie Davis (10)	46
Elen Brown (11)	47
Alfie Jordan (11)	48
Jake Smith (9)	49
Daniel Phillips (10)	50
Cassie Saunders (9)	51
Imogen George (10)	52
Naomi Saunders (11)	53
Tomos Ramsden (10)	54
Ben Willingham (9)	55
Elijah John Coles (9)	56
Eloise Lawn (9)	57
Lana Hartley (10)	58
Lottie Steel (10)	59
Beth Washbourne (10)	60
Bradley Edmunds (11)	61
Lucy Blyth (10)	62
George Harrop-Griffiths (11)	63
Erin Jones (9)	64

Sara Angharad Pember (10)	65
Auzair Khan (10)	66
Elliot Downing (9)	67
Siân Lorna Jones (9)	68
Noah Morris (10)	69
Freddie Wilsher-Swann (10)	70
Daniel Willingham (11)	71
Freya Brown (10)	72
Izzy May (11)	73
Ffion Brooks (10)	74
Mathimenan Ragavan (11)	75
Hannah Pugsley (10)	76
James Harrop-Griffiths (9)	77
Caitlin Jeremiah (9)	78
Tomas Francis (9)	79

Broadhempston Primary School, Totnes

Vera Kirby (7)	80
Evan Craven (9)	81
Tessa Jones (7)	82
Mabel Kirby (10)	83
Sola-Mae Handelsman-Bryant (9)	84

Courtlands Special School, Plymouth

Leo Williams (10)	85
Jemma Saundry (10)	86
Leighton Daly (10)	88
Courtney Hancock (10)	89
Louis Horne (10)	90
Alfie Cox (10)	91
Daniel Burt (10)	92
Caleb Malloch (10)	93
Wei-Heng Beh (11)	94
Drew Morshead (9)	95
Mason John Bittle (9)	96
Lucas Middleton (11)	97
Benjamin Richard Seaborne (10)	98
Jack Jackson (10)	99
Darran Roberts (10)	100

Ellis MacIntosh (9)	101
Kian Peart (9)	102
Christopher Hallam (9)	103
Lola Ann Nutbean (10)	104
Jasmine Saundry (9)	105
George Davies (9)	106
Flynn Beal (9)	107

Gotherington Primary School, Cheltenham

Daniel Lee (11)	108
Kate Coldwell (11)	109
Freya Lindgren (10)	110
Lily Marchant (11)	111
Jesse Elizabeth Steel (9)	112
Amelia Freeman (10)	113
Dylan Kingswood (9)	114
Katie Marsh (10)	115
Huw Evans (10)	116

Sheringham Primary School, London

Manfoosah Maria Begum (7)	117
Nene Isatou Jallow (8)	118
Ashir Imran (8)	119
Madeeha Rahman (8)	120
Iqra Miah (7)	121
Leeana Tahiyyah (8)	122
Afifa Nuzha (8)	123
Hamdaan Hussain (7)	124
Enos Eyassu (8)	125
Ajwah Qasim (7)	126
Jay Singh Sommers (7)	127
Meerab Fouz Butt (8)	128

St Anthony's School For Girls, London

Aurelia Westlake (8)	129
Romilly Burgess (7)	130
Helena Mayo (8)	131
Macy Lehmann (7)	132

Irem Cenkci (7)	133
Ellie Davidson (7)	134
Carlotta Bruno (8)	135

St Edward's Catholic Primary School, London

Meagan Jade Sanchez (11)	136
Jayla Jayne Jara (10)	138
Melanie Alphonse (10)	139
Genoveva Martin (10)	140
Chelsea Angeles (10)	141
Kassandra Mae Delos Reyes (9)	142
Paul Manzon (10)	143
Divine Okua (8)	144
Tessa Agnes Arun (10)	145
Ozi Daisy-Divine Oparaugo (8)	146
Angel Nana Achiaa Asamoah (11)	147
Chienyemona Wright (11)	148
Nayara Simoes (9)	149
Darren Guba (10)	150
Olivia Nkili Molokwu (10)	151
Ezekiel Clement (9)	152

St Mary's RC Primary School, London

Phillip Wayne Torres (9)	153
Nevaeh Harris (11)	154
Charmelle Eligado (9)	156
Dorien Ortutai-Hughes (7)	158
Sean George Murphy (10)	160
Chloe Jessica Cummins (10)	161
David Waldoch (10)	162
Jerrimae De Vera (10)	163
Keira Dugasse (10)	164
Joshua De Sousa (11)	165
Lawrence Pascua (10)	166
Euan Castillo (10)	167
Ashley Oliveira Pereira Da Silva (11)	168
Christina Panisales (11)	169
Wintana Dawit (10)	170

Freya-Lee O'Dea (11)	171
Hanneka Cabantes (10)	172
Jazmine Ali (10)	173
Marcel Jnolewis (10)	174
Daisy Gonzalez (11)	175
Carlee-Jane Senorin (8)	176
Adriana Da Silva (11)	177
Megan Ellen Conway-Faulds (11)	178
Shanola Toussaint-Soaga (10)	179
Gina Paiva Godinho (10)	180
Cameron Williams (11)	181
Jazmin O'Brien (10)	182
Savannah Martin-Lansiquot (11)	183
Layla Harris (7)	184
Skye Harris (10)	185

St Matthias CE Primary School, London

Heba Bouzerar (9)	186
Tayler Campbelle Clarck (10)	187
Lorenzo Perzhilla (9)	188
Khaiden Kentebe (10)	189
Tilly Latham (9)	190
Shanique Titer (9)	191
Mariya Ahmed (10)	192
Ericka Kasongo (9)	193
Saffa Ahmed (10)	194

St Vincent De Paul RC Primary School, London

Darren Kwo (11)	195
Josh Herbie Pritchard (11)	196
Giulia Caturano (10)	198
Fred Del Cerro (11)	199
Sally-Ann Forrest (10)	200
Bianca Polloni (10)	201
Jamie Eson-Benjamin (10)	202
Mia Moreschi (11)	203
Ruby Ella Carton (10)	204

THE POEMS

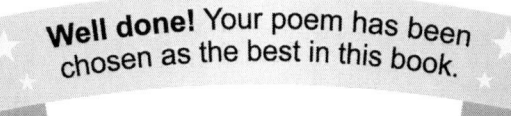

Well done! Your poem has been chosen as the best in this book.

The Haunted House

The creak of the floorboards,
The squeak of the stair,
As you go up and down,
You hear the clunk of the chair.

The spike of the nails,
The spooky tails of the rats,
The hardness of the carpet,
The creepy wings of the bats.

The glimpse of an eerie ghost,
The flicker of a candle
About to go out
The squeaking of a door handle.

The dip of the bed,
As I gently lay my head,
The coolness of the air
Even though there is nobody there.

The scream from a deafening ear
This area seems out of bounds
Then I wake up,
But it is all safe and sound!

Pippa Cudmore (10)
Gotherington Primary School, Cheltenham

The Dragon In My Dreams

His eyes, deep dark and seething,
He guards his cave with rumbling breathing
When the sun falls he begins his hunt for the evening

His menacing claws reach out for the cliff side
He beadily spots his prey down by the tide,
He swoops and snatches his feast which does abide.

Like thundering rain he swoops and falls,
Keen for more food he roars and calls.
Don't let him see you or he'll send you to your pall.

With scaled vermilion wings he boasts,
Feel his breath, he's coming close.
When you hear his roar, you know,
You're toast!

Megan Sarfas (11)

The Mystical Madhouse

Oh snow-white Caladrius please come back,
Such wonders are discovered when flying on your back,
The fairies are prancing and the dancers dancing,
And the dinosaurs stomping about,
It's chaos here it's like a madhouse!

The pirates are locked in cells,
And the wizards casting spells,
The monsters are looming in the fog,
And Superman had to bring home a dog!

The supermodels are strutting,
And the writers tutting,
Oh please come home Caladrius,
I know you're out there,
I want you back you're my big, protective bear.

Mia Cleave (10)

Untitled

There's a monster on my ceiling.
Her eyes are green as green grass freshly blowing in the wind.
Her ears are as wavy as branches swishing in the summer sun.
Her fangs small as an ant scampering under a dirty old log.
Her wings are as huge as the London Eye going back and forward in the nice hot spring day.
Her claws are as sharp as a can opener carving through steel and metal.
Her tail is as curly as a snail shell going very slow on the meadow, and her name was Ouvano!

Lily May Elizabeth Ormerod (9)

Sweet Dreams

S ail off to Dreamland
W here all your dreams will come true
E veryone in Dreamland is really nice
E very night is an adventure
T here you make the rules

D ream clouds dance across the night sky
R emember, you never have to say goodbye
E ven when you're old and grey
A ll it takes is imagination
M aybe you will see me there

In your sweet dreams!

Hannah Jayne Bennett (10)

All About My Dream

M y dream takes place in a faraway land
Y ou can go there as well

D reams can come true
R ecreate my life as a fantasy
E verlasting
A ll my fears wash away
M y dream is amazing!

This is my dream.

Grace Eve Bennett (10)

Space

S aturn, stars shine as bright as the sun
P attern in the galaxy everywhere
A ir lock you can see all of Saturn's greatness.
C ubes floating from all directions
E ating wonderful space food.

Rio Williams (9)

The Silver Stallion

'Who are you?' I ask.
Peering out of my windowsill,
A dashing silver stallion atop the winding hill.
As I approach really carefully.
The horse said with a smile, 'Come on I'll give you the ride of your life, I promise it will be worthwhile.
We can canter and gallop over the hills and maybe just a gentle walk,'
'But hold on,' I said rubbing my eyes, 'did you just talk? OK I will,' I said, grabbing my tack, 'but just wait, are we riding like this or bareback?'
'A saddle and a bridle is just not for me, as you can see, Abbey, I was born free.'
I jumped on his back and threw my tack,
I won't be needing any more of that.
We cantered and galloped and I spotted a sign with a tiny piece of grime,
it said: 'Just ten minutes',
But I was too busy listening to the crickets.
When we got back it was peaceful, Wow I never rode bareback before,
Then, the slight sound of a creaking door.
I knew it was time that goodbyes were said,
I suddenly woke up in bed.

Abbey Amelia Broome (9)
Aberdare Town CW Primary School, Aberdare

Star Of The Screen

Lights, camera, action!
That's what I want to hear.
I'd love to be an actress,
Even for just a year!

Horror films are my favourite,
I like a good old scare.
I want to play a spooky ghost,
So scaredy-cats beware!

I love to practise all my lines,
And sing and dance along
It's Hollywood I'm aiming for,
It's right where I belong.

I'd love my name in the credits
of the best film you've ever seen.
My dad thinks I'll get there,
because he says I'm a drama queen!

Nerys Stocks (9)
Aberdare Town CW Primary School, Aberdare

The Alien And Me!

There it was, the Principality Stadium,
But then I spotted an alien
It was very green
And it looked like the queen,
But it was posher than Bradley Walsh at the Palladium.

So then I just went for it.
It started to run a little bit,
Then I went a bit faster
Because I ate pasta
This made me really fit.

So I ran and ran
Until I saw Dan
I passed it out
And had a clout.
Then I said to Dan, 'Do you think we beat them man?'

Corey James Hansford (9)
Aberdare Town CW Primary School, Aberdare

All Different Aliens

A liens are different as you can tell
L ots of different colours, lots of different smells
I wonder if it's true, if aliens are lurking around through space
E very alien has a lot of fun, playing games and drinking squash
N oisy aliens go to bed. Sleep all night and dream of eating naughty boys for breakfast.

Ffion Harris Stark (8)
Aberdare Town CW Primary School, Aberdare

World's Best Player

Messi is one of the world's best players;
Better than Pele you say?
He skills defenders like they are not there,
And even has time to fix his hair.
He wears the captain armband with pride
When he lost against Chile he cried.
Most games he can snatch
Then win Man of the Match!

Lucas Jesse Burford (9)
Aberdare Town CW Primary School, Aberdare

Aliens

A liens have different colours, some look different too
L ots of aliens can be nice or bad sometimes
I can see aliens running across the woods
E very small alien is funny and silly
N aughty aliens are nosey and get up to mischief, oh dear!

Morgan Matthews (8)
Aberdare Town CW Primary School, Aberdare

Fairies Are My Friends!

F airies are my friends
A s I wake up
I n the middle of the night
R oaming in my garden
I see a fairy, set to fly
E choing in the starry night
S he then flew off into the shimmering light.

Carys Jones (9)
Aberdare Town CW Primary School, Aberdare

The Loud Volume

The loud volume of the bass drum,
And the humming from the choir.
And the soft Christmas lullaby.
Listen to the strumming of the guitar.
Listen to that tooting of the trumpet.
Why not change the beat again.
Listen to that neat refrain.

Kaitlyn Butterfill (8)
Aberdare Town CW Primary School, Aberdare

Magic

M onsters float into my head
A s I close my eyes in bed
G hosts and goblins come to play
I think of all I did that day
C ount from one to ten, then I am awake.

Hudson Blake Griffiths (9)
Aberdare Town CW Primary School, Aberdare

Aliens

A liens are different colours
L ots of aliens in space
I ntelligent aliens everywhere
E very alien is so amazing
N oisy aliens everywhere.

Emmie Sayce-Edwards (8)
Aberdare Town CW Primary School, Aberdare

Magical Music

Drumming drums so strong and loud,
The sound it makes is fast and proud,
A soft and soothing bright guitar,
The sound it makes is like a star.

Sophie Harries (8)
Aberdare Town CW Primary School, Aberdare

I Can See The Wonderful World

I can see great green leaves
I can see a magical rainbow
I can see the salty sea
I can see the terrific trees
I can see the bright sun.

Jake Berry (8)
Aberdare Town CW Primary School, Aberdare

Magic Instruments

I can hear the big booming bass guitar
I can hear the cool calming clarinet
I can hear the big booming drum
I can hear the tweeting birds.

Morgan Evans (8)
Aberdare Town CW Primary School, Aberdare

All About Magic

M agic is a miracle
A ll around the globe
G adgets for experiments
I n the lab with the science
C at.

Anna-Louise Grafham (9)
Aberdare Town CW Primary School, Aberdare

I Can Hear

I can hear the smooth saxophone.
I can hear the booming big drum.
I can hear the deep double bass.
I can hear the strum of the guitar.

Ewan Milton (8)
Aberdare Town CW Primary School, Aberdare

Aliens

A liens are coming
L ightning strikes
I nsane strikes
E ggs with aliens inside
N inja turtles.

Owen Lynam (8)
Aberdare Town CW Primary School, Aberdare

Aliens

A liens
L earn about aliens
I love aliens
E very alien is cool
N aughty aliens everywhere.

Kieran Rodda (8)
Aberdare Town CW Primary School, Aberdare

The I Can See Poem

I can see blazing red fire
I can see chirping on the autumn trees.
I can see beautiful art
I can see really nice friends.

Tylor Sweet (8)
Aberdare Town CW Primary School, Aberdare

I Can See

I can see the salty River Thames
I can see adorable puppy pugs
I can see autumn leaves
I can see a magic rainbow.

Madison Eve Shellard (8)
Aberdare Town CW Primary School, Aberdare

Alien Poem

I can see a savage alien
I can see a gigantic alien.
I can see a slobbery alien
I can see a very big gold alien.

Kian Meyrick (8)
Aberdare Town CW Primary School, Aberdare

Untitled

I can hear a big booming bass bassoon
I can hear the whistle of a recorder
I can hear a tiny lovely ping of a piano.

Owen North (8)
Aberdare Town CW Primary School, Aberdare

I Can See

I can see autumnal leaves
I can see amazing people
I can see fire camp
I can see an azure ocean.

Ethan Carey (8)
Aberdare Town CW Primary School, Aberdare

My Nightmare

N ightmare, I had a nightmare last night, it was really scary; I had an army of pirates, my family were there as well.

I was a wizard fighting against fire-breathing dragons, ice wizards, terrifying sabre-tooth tigers and T-rexes.

G ave me a fright; woke me up in the middle of the night; smoke on the battlefield of Saturn.

H igh in the air fighting with my wizardry spells against evil forces with an army. Freaky!

T omorrow awaits, I must fight for tomorrow will allies against opponents

M any pirates and athletes died, then out of nowhere friendly monsters came to help me in war.

A nd I told my family to fly as far away as possible. A massive T-rex leapt over, I zapped it - dead. Phew!

R eading the newspaper was a man in Trafalgar Square, London. He got hit by the rocket and it blew up.

E veryone on Saturn died (even me) because it hit another planet that hit the sun and blew it up.

Jacob Lee (10)
Archbishop Rowan Williams (VA) CIW Primary School, Caldicot

Look! It's A Flying Cat!

Look! It's a flying cat!
With his midnight blue hat,
his green eyes glistening with sparkles.
As he gazed into the sunlit sky,
with a hint of purple,
in the soft clouds.

His fellow friend,
the unicorn,
just beside him.
His golden tip horn,
guiding us through,
a coat as white as snow.
A multicoloured tail,
swishing in the cooling breeze.

The wind,
brushing my face,
wiping my worries away.
A sky filled with colours,
dancing in song.

A golden arrow,
darts through the sky,
piercing the silence,
with a whistle and a...
Whoosh!

Missing us,
not by much.
Then vanished,
Into the night sky.

A question ran through my head,
like dancing angels.
Can we go back to Dream World?
With a *click, click, click,*
of the unicorn horn,
we were off!
Heading for the horizon.

As I slept on the fluffy
unicorn's back,
with a pounding heart,
slowly drooping,
I suddenly knew that the best of dreams has to come
to an end.

Arwen Skinner (10)
Archbishop Rowan Williams (VA) CIW Primary School, Caldicot

The Dreaded Dream Of Time

One cold, dark night I had a fright.
In my head was the place that I dread,
I dived into 1945, I'm in a place in Berlin.
I'm drenched in a trench with the US and British army,
and next to me, a fat rat.

I'm cold and wet and miserable but then I'm at
the 2012 Olympics and it's the cycling!
But I don't get to see the end of it because I'm
abducted...
by a UFO!

But then I'm in a room with a clown,
I feel as if I'm going to drown,
in the depths of fear.

I'm running as fast as a deer, up and down,
away from the clown.
But then I smell smoke,
I poke myself to see if I'm back.
No, I look outside.

I hear screams and I smell smoke.
This wasn't a joke!
I hear the roar of flames,

inside my dreams; I can see the glowing flare of fire,
then I awake with a quake,
and I rest for the best.

Kieran Howells (11)
Archbishop Rowan Williams (VA) CIW Primary School, Caldicot

Animation Star

As I step into a world of imagination,
I realise I have turned into animation.
I wander around the fun-filled studio,
then I see a familiar face.

I see his head,
popping up from out of the blue.
I know him,
It's nothing new.

With his big shiny eyes,
his appearance it's no surprise.
The character I see is Mickey Mouse,
the joyful fun one, from the clubhouse.

He shows me all the rooms,
and introduces me to all the famous cartoons
Minnie, Pluto and Goofy too...
I like the new world,
It's pretty cool.

Now we're about to be on TV,
I open my mouth about to speak,
but no sound comes out.
Not even a squeak!

Just then I wake up in my bed,
sweat trickling down my head.
I liked that dream,
it was fun.
But I guess all the enjoyable fun is done.

Erin Beasley (10)
Archbishop Rowan Williams (VA) CIW Primary School, Caldicot

Flying Through A Dream

My eyes shut,
I drift off to my own world.
I lay there curled up and warm.
I stand high on a hill,
the whispering wind blows through my hair,
fresh air fills my lungs.

At the bottom of the hill is an ocean,
big and blue,
sparkling in the horizon.

My feet lift,
I slowly, slowly begin to drift.
Higher and higher I go,
I feel as light as a feather.
Soaring through the sky,
higher than the birds.

Dipping and diving,
looping and swooping.
I feel as free as a bird,
gliding through the dancing clouds.

I start going down, down, down,
and I slowly reach the ground.

My feet dig into the sand,
as the sun hits my skin.

I wake up happy and peaceful.
The sun shone brightly through my curtains.
Sadly my dream has gone.

Charley Rockliffe-Fidler (10)
Archbishop Rowan Williams (VA) CIW Primary School, Caldicot

We Got To The Finish!

I dreamed a dream in bed last night,
of places most bizarre,
of buses flying in and out,
and wind that goes *baa!*

One of those buses was of course mine.
Mine was all different.
It had a cow that goes *Ka! Ka!*
And a bird that goes *Moo!*

We crashed into a house as big as space,
a giant alien walked towards me.
He opened the door and made a race,
my Double Decker KitKat verses his amazing low rider.

We made an agreement on whoever reaches the moon first,
must put a flag on there to win.
Half way through we crashed an amazing crash.
We broke our engine but the cow fixed it.

We had to get in front of the amazing low rider,
so, step on the lemonade boosters
We had a siren telling everyone to get out of the way.
Yay! We got to the moon first.

Iwan James Hall (10)
Archbishop Rowan Williams (VA) CIW Primary School, Caldicot

The Dream

There once was a big land called Dream,
Where lots of people started to beam.
They started to clash,
away they did dash,
Then they were all falling into a stream.
They started to fall through the clouds,
and had a couple of bad rows.
How do they do it?
Do they try to knit?
These people probably have mouths!
Then one big day the dragons came,
they wanted to try to find them a name.
Many thought to pray
Then they said, 'You must pay!'
However, they just wanted fame.
After that day in history,
It was known as the mystery.
Everyone to this day,
celebrates the event in May,
telling each other the odd story.

Lucy Nicholson (10)
Archbishop Rowan Williams (VA) CIW Primary School, Caldicot

Dragon Maker

I had a dream last night,
but different from the rest.
This one stood out.
A friendly dragon was there.

He was big and tall with huge scales;
his fire was as hot as the sun.
His feet sizzled in the sunlight;
his eyes looked at me as if to say hi.

Then he knelt down next to me,
I got onto his back and went to dragon world.
Every type of dragon was there
Big to small.

There were flying cats and burping trees,
then he put me down and I started to fade away.

Then I woke up,
I looked around me everything was fine.
My candle flickered as if it were dancing.
Then next to me was my toy dragon,
his friends, and a cat.

From then I knew it was all a dream,
from what I had seen.
My toys fell and made a bang,
As the birds sang.

Nia Davies (10)
Archbishop Rowan Williams (VA) CIW Primary School, Caldicot

My Teacher's Having A Bad Day

This is a strange poem; my teacher is having a bit of a bad day.
Her brother has bitten her bottom (he is a dragon),
But my teacher has super powers, re-growing her bottom.
Her brother gets angry and shouts, 'I will bite it off again!'
Their mum comes bursting in with penguins as bodyguards.
She marches them back to their home in the clouds.
My teacher's brother pushes her off the cloud.
Now my teacher's a wolf, meet Red Riding Hood.
Red is not happy, whips a knife from her knickers.
This is the end of my teacher.

Harvey Lewis Heaven (10)
Archbishop Rowan Williams (VA) CIW Primary School, Caldicot

That Magical Day

I was waiting patiently ready to go on holiday until...
We start going into the atmosphere and hit an asteroid, *crash!*
I go ploughing through the sky and hit land called Neverland, *whoosh!*
When I woke up I saw black smoke everywhere,
I go exploring for ages.
Then I find a bush; it makes a rattle!
As I go through it.
As I walk through I hear music.
When I got to the other side I saw dancing fairies dancing around the fire, *twirl!*
I get hit with a spark; I realised it was all just a dream!

Xavi-Mai Taylor (11)
Archbishop Rowan Williams (VA) CIW Primary School, Caldicot

Superheroes

There once was a Superhero called Sam,
who thought he was sUper cool.
He said, 'I am here to save People.'
He knew Everone loved him,
Until one day when he felt Really sad.
Another superHero had come along,
whose name was Eric
He made everyone Really like him,
So Sam cried, 'Oh what a pity,'
As he returned homE, very upset.
Trying to find a Solution to his dilemma.

Archie Davis (10)
Archbishop Rowan Williams (VA) CIW Primary School, Caldicot

Sweets, Chocolate And Candy

C ame home and went to bed and had a dream about Candy Land!
A dmire the chocolate and sweets in Candy Land!
N o healthy stuff, just amazing in Candy Land
D on't be scared, dig in, it is amazing in Candy Land!
Y ummy in my belly in Candy Land! It's amazing!

L oop the loop Candy Land! Is amazing
A mazing chocolate and sweets in Candy Land!
N ever say no to Candy Land!
D on't forget it is just a dream... awww!

Elen Brown (11)
Archbishop Rowan Williams (VA) CIW Primary School, Caldicot

Zombies And Clowns Give Billy A Nightmare

N ightmares happened and I was frightened
I was being chased by zombies and clowns
G oodness me, I was horrified
H appening to fall over, they almost caught me
T he zombies and clowns were catching up
M y! I have had no nightmare like this before
A nd they were about to catch me
R eality was so real in this nightmare
E *nd this nightmare*, I thought to myself, until they caught me, that was when my nightmare ended.

Alfie Jordan (11)
Archbishop Rowan Williams (VA) CIW Primary School, Caldicot

Dragons

D ragons are friendly. There are different kinds - ice, fire, water, grass
R oaming in the wild you can find them in caves and forests
A ll of the dragons started fighting, but first they'd been friendly
G rass started to die because the dragons were fighting
O n the roof tops they fought all day and all night
N ice people were getting really angry at the dragons
S tartled by peoples reaction, the dragons decided to become friends again.

Jake Smith (9)
Archbishop Rowan Williams (VA) CIW Primary School, Caldicot

Wizard Spells

Wondrous wizarding wisdom
Incredible intelligent beings.
Zigzags of lightning peak through the clouds.
You must Always obey your wizarding lord,
They Redeem their powers like heroes
Damaging your rivals to win.

Super Sonic sins
They are the Peacekeepers.
Exquisite spells,
Lethal powers,
Landscape of Lightning.
Spectacular Spells.

Daniel Phillips (10)
Archbishop Rowan Williams (VA) CIW Primary School, Caldicot

Dancer

I was Dancing like a ballerina, everyone watching me in the competition.
I was on my horse when another Amazing horse rider told me I was really good.
That Night I was thinking that I *could* be a real dancer too.
In my dreams I would dance in a Club, but my mum had no faith in me.
UnExpectedly, a young man asked me to join him later in the dance hall.
It was the horse Rider; he'd seen into my future career.

Cassie Saunders (9)
Archbishop Rowan Williams (VA) CIW Primary School, Caldicot

My Special Place

I am in a village in Italy with my very best friends,
And our special friendship never ends.
We've just found some kittens with fluffy tails,
And some sweet little birds that are actually quails.
In our village in Italy, quails are rare,
You can usually find them eating a pear.
But birds like crows are easy to find,
You usually find them pecking at rind.
Now that's my story, my wonderful dream,
But it actually ends with me eating ice cream.

Imogen George (10)
Archbishop Rowan Williams (VA) CIW Primary School, Caldicot

Candyland

C andy cane window frames taste so good
A nd green jelly beans for grass
N ever say never to candy in Candy Land
D on't be afraid, take whatever you like
Y ou'll never be alone, someone's always there

L and with green and white fondant hills with candy on top
A nd clouds made of thick eclair
N o one ever dares to leave
D on't forget it's just a dream.

Naomi Saunders (11)
Archbishop Rowan Williams (VA) CIW Primary School, Caldicot

Racing Driver

R isking; people are so brave
A lways try to win the race
C ars are so very fast
I n a world of their own
N ot worrying about others who drive
G ot to go, pedal to the metal.

D runk driving is not allowed,
R acing they find so fun
I think they do their best
V ery dangerous job to have
E veryone can take part
R eady, steady go, go, go!

Tomos Ramsden (10)
Archbishop Rowan Williams (VA) CIW Primary School, Caldicot

Four Greek Gods ~ Haikus

Zeus
Loud, thunder booming
He's very strong and mighty.
The king of the gods.

Poseidon
Waves are crashing down
No more surfing for today
He's the earth shaker.

Hades
He's lord of the dead
Ruler of the underworld
He controls the dead.

Apollo
God of poetry
He's the real music man with
Great archery skills.

Ben Willingham (9)
Archbishop Rowan Williams (VA) CIW Primary School, Caldicot

The Adventure

A trip to the woods
D own to the forest where the creatures live
V ery deep in the heart of the forest
E veryone there goes hunting for Phoebe the Phoenix
N o-one found Phoebe the Phoenix in the woods
T he phoenix was lost, somewhere in the woods.
U nder the leaves she hid from the hunters
R evealing herself to no one
E veryone, passing her by, unnoticed!

Elijah John Coles (9)
Archbishop Rowan Williams (VA) CIW Primary School, Caldicot

Dreams

The magic dreams fly through the thin air,
nice dreams come to those who love and care.
Children will dream of fairies and despair.
The light of the dark and the dark of the light.
Gather around to bring the night,
stars shine like bright diamonds, for those in need and in fright.
The daylight arrives to cover up fears,
darkness hopes it will spread out to everyone near.
Wait silently, watch, look, hear.

Eloise Lawn (9)
Archbishop Rowan Williams (VA) CIW Primary School, Caldicot

Once Upon A Dream

Once upon a dream...
I was with my friends walking through the grass,
when suddenly, all my worries pass.
When I'm with my friends I have no care in the world.
Suddenly we are lost, amongst some trees and frost,
the ice glistened against the rocks.
Once upon a dream.
Once upon a dream there were creatures with wings,
and ogres that sings.
No matter how long I spend, this dream will never end.

Lana Hartley (10)
Archbishop Rowan Williams (VA) CIW Primary School, Caldicot

Flying With Peter Pan

Whoosh!
Up into the sky;
the sky is a black blanket.
Peter Pan is with me,
by my side.
I feel like I am a bird,
flying through the sky.
The stardust keeps me up,
going through Netherland.
While the trees dance,
the sea stays calm.
I am a feather whizzing through.
The air while the air swept past my ears quickly!
Then suddenly I glide, back into my cosy bed.

Lottie Steel (10)
Archbishop Rowan Williams (VA) CIW Primary School, Caldicot

Through The Mirror!

Through the mirror lays a magical place.
Can you imagine?
Through the mirror the sky is bright; it wouldn't be fulfilled without its dazzling light.
Can you imagine?
Through the mirror there are magical creatures that lay under a spell.
Can you imagine?
Through the mirror lays all my friends locked away to keep the spell at bay.
Till never end the curse will stay.
Can you imagine?

Beth Washbourne (10)
Archbishop Rowan Williams (VA) CIW Primary School, Caldicot

The Street Race

I am the richest man in Australia:
I am in my Lamborghini Adventador (LP750-4) and £100,000!
If I lose the street race then my cash and ride goes to the winner.
As I drift around the corner; I hear my fans cheering my name.
I get to the first place... Oh No!
As I back down to second place it all fades away I wake up.
'Bradley, Bradley, wake up its morning!'

Bradley Edmunds (11)
Archbishop Rowan Williams (VA) CIW Primary School, Caldicot

Deep Dark Fears

As I close my eyes, darkness fills the night sky.
Stars shoot across the sky as quick as bolts of lightning
Then all of a sudden I'm in a cave,
a cave full of bats, lots of them.

Bats with jagged wings,
bats with fangs as sharp as a knife!
Sleeping soundly throughout the night.
As I walk backwards, I trip over something,
Did it just move?

Lucy Blyth (10)
Archbishop Rowan Williams (VA) CIW Primary School, Caldicot

Nightmare

N ice sunny day
I t was all calm
G oodness I'm falling
H elpless as I was spinning
T here was nothing but darkness
M oments before I hit the ground
A light begins to shine
R eady to hit the ground but before I do...
E xcitement fills me when I land. It's soft and comfy and light is all around.

George Harrop-Griffiths (11)
Archbishop Rowan Williams (VA) CIW Primary School, Caldicot

Pancakes

P ancakes are irresistible
A ll pancakes are super yummy
N either plain nor spicy; the toppings, they're still incredible
C ream is the best topping
A ll people should have lots of pancakes each day
K ittens love munching on them
E ven with fruit they're outstanding
S it down and take a bite or two!

Erin Jones (9)
Archbishop Rowan Williams (VA) CIW Primary School, Caldicot

The Frightful Forest

In the deep, dark forest the monster lies,
squelching through the mud waiting for a big surprise.
I hear a loud snoring from the other side,
I see a huge foot right before my eyes.
Running as quick as a flash to the cliff side,
I come to the edge and shout goodbye!
No more worries now,
I'm actually in my bed, staring at the night sky.

Sara Angharad Pember (10)
Archbishop Rowan Williams (VA) CIW Primary School, Caldicot

A Young Boy With Superpowers

There once was a young boy named Greg,
He was very happy in bed.
He had superpowers,
And slept the day for hours.
He fought crimes all night, so he said!

Greg saved the day, then he saw Ginger!
Greg chased him, then he was a ninja!
He was a funny friend,
and he fought to the end,
His friend was a very good pincher.

Auzair Khan (10)
Archbishop Rowan Williams (VA) CIW Primary School, Caldicot

Funny Football

Once there was a nasty, horrible octopus,
who played football with all legs!
He dreamt of playing in the world cup,
however, he couldn't tie his laces up.

He always fell over,
and his team mates laughed.
Until one match day,
he surprised them all!

When he stumbled and scored...
The winning goal!

Elliot Downing (9)
Archbishop Rowan Williams (VA) CIW Primary School, Caldicot

The Happy Witch

Once there was a lovely young witch,
Who fell down in a dark, muddy ditch,
She was a nice girl
She wore some nice pearls,
Though they soon disappeared in that ditch.

That lovely witch loved to make
Really big, fat juicy cakes.
She had her birthday
In the month of May,
And she really did love to bake.

Siân Lorna Jones (9)
Archbishop Rowan Williams (VA) CIW Primary School, Caldicot

Pet Heroes

There was a superhero called Doug,
his sidekick pet was a giant pug.
They flew across lands
to fight giant hands,
So they could get the majestic jug.

And so the pet heroes saved the day,
Oh no! It's the enemy called Jay,
he lives in a bin,
His friend is called Tim,
The enemies are now eating hay.

Noah Morris (10)
Archbishop Rowan Williams (VA) CIW Primary School, Caldicot

A British Man

There once was a man in Great Britain,
Who owned a wonderful kitten.
He went to see Rex,
Who was a T-rex,
And gave him a pair of warm mittens.

The man from Britain was a wizard,
He had loads and loads of lizards.
He once bought a lamb,
Who ate his friend Sam,
Till all that was left was his gizzard.

Freddie Wilsher-Swann (10)
Archbishop Rowan Williams (VA) CIW Primary School, Caldicot

Candy Land

C andy all around me everywhere
A ll I can see is candy
N o one around, so more for me
D elicious candy everywhere
Y ou've seen more candy

L ots and lots of candy
A ll I can see is candy
N o one around so more for me
D elicious candy everywhere.

Daniel Willingham (11)
Archbishop Rowan Williams (VA) CIW Primary School, Caldicot

Fairies

F riendly little magic men flying around
A dorable tiny, magic winged creatures
I ncredibly sweet
R are things soaring through the air
I ndependent, tiny minds.
E asily distracted; busy working.
S haring their magical wishes.

Freya Brown (10)
Archbishop Rowan Williams (VA) CIW Primary School, Caldicot

Magical Mythical Dreams

I had a dream one night ago,
Fairies dancing among the snow.
Dreams are strange things,
Can't you see they're mystic, they're magic?
They're weird, even to me!
Unicorns flying in the sky, their beauty will never tell a lie.

Izzy May (11)
Archbishop Rowan Williams (VA) CIW Primary School, Caldicot

The Terrifying Spider

There once was a young girl who wanted to work in a zoo,
to work in the reptile house, but there was a problem.
There, in the middle of the room was...
A freaky spider,
waiting for her, waiting to pounce.
Could she ever go back?

Ffion Brooks (10)
Archbishop Rowan Williams (VA) CIW Primary School, Caldicot

Mario

Luigi Green Toad
Toad is captured by Bowser.
Bradley's pet dragon
scared, terrified, help!
Pixelated characters,
Video game boss.

Retro video,
Game consoles are fun to play.
It's me Mario!

Mathimenan Ragavan (11)
Archbishop Rowan Williams (VA) CIW Primary School, Caldicot

Ballet

B alancing on the ball of one foot,
A mazing control
L ight spotlights land on me!
L oads of performances to do!
E xams are coming,
T urns are fast and entertaining.

Hannah Pugsley (10)
Archbishop Rowan Williams (VA) CIW Primary School, Caldicot

Funky Monkey

There once was a very big monkey
who always tried to be funky.
He was friends with a clown
who wore a dressing gown,
but this made him look very chunky.

James Harrop-Griffiths (9)
Archbishop Rowan Williams (VA) CIW Primary School, Caldicot

The Dancer

There once was a very good dancer,
Who had dreams to be the best prancer.
She was very funny,
Making loads of money.
She was a magnificent bouncer!

Caitlin Jeremiah (9)
Archbishop Rowan Williams (VA) CIW Primary School, Caldicot

Present Poem

P rofessionals
R epeat
E xtreme
S cience
E xperiments
N eeding
T ime and perseverance.

Tomas Francis (9)
Archbishop Rowan Williams (VA) CIW Primary School, Caldicot

Dream In A Jar

I was here one moment and there the next.
My heart was beating like a drum.
I already knew what I'd become.
I was in the world of dream.
The glass around me did nothing but gleam.
I was in a big glass jar!
People around me played the guitar.
Suddenly a man all dressed in black,
he came right round the crowd at the back,
strangely he then turned from black to blue.
My worst fear had come true.
It was him!
Creeping closer and closer coming to get me
The nightmare!

Vera Kirby (7)
Broadhempston Primary School, Totnes

Dreams Are Amazing

Dreams have a lot in common.
We all have them once in a while.
Some of them are very short.
And some dreams can last for hours.
Sometimes we dream nightmares.
And sometimes don't ever dream at all.
Mice in little holes race away then you become a mouse.
Eggs smell like delicious bacon pasties.
New dreams with clowns, Dinosaurs and then I see some monsters.
Guns, swords and I'm about to get killed...
Finally I'm out from my nightmare and I'm thrilled!

Evan Craven (9)
Broadhempston Primary School, Totnes

Dream Pony

D is for dapples of spots on pony's soft fur
R is for riding so fast the world is a blur
E is for eating apples and sharing the cores
A is for adventures on the misty moors
M is for mountains to ride

P is for pony who never gets tired
O is for oxygen for the new foals
N is for no jumping poles
Y is for yee-ha! Riding so fast.

Tessa Jones (7)
Broadhempston Primary School, Totnes

The Dream Drifter

In this dream world I can't decide
Whether I'm drifting there or drifting back like the tide
A sea of sun and a sky of ground,
I don't know where my feet will be found,
As up and down aren't your usual sky and ground,
A million ideas are squashed into one.
This place is a paradise of fun,
My eyes are open to stay asleep
In this dream I will keep!

Mabel Kirby (10)
Broadhempston Primary School, Totnes

Foxy Flopsy

My dear old Foxy Flopsy,
Foxy Flopsy climbed a tree and couldn't get down.
But did that stop me? No!
So I climbed the tree myself, but it wasn't low.
I climbed the tree to halfway,
But Foxy Flopsy was at the top.
At that point we both were stuck.
So I called the police, but they were at the pub, getting a pug!

Sola-Mae Handelsman-Bryant (9)
Broadhempston Primary School, Totnes

Nottingham Castle

It was a lovely day in Nottingham.
The sun was as bright as lava.
The king and queen were waiting for other royalty,
The knights' loyalty is to the king and queen.
The guards are slurping then they are burping.
The gentle wind blew through the castle.
The king and queen were sharing a banquet with other royalty.
The captain of the knights approached the king and queen.
A royal song began.

The gunpowder went with a *bang, bang!*
The people in the castle and the village went with a shock
They thought they were under attack
The king and queen are back from the banquet.
The king said, 'We aren't under attack, it's the gunpowder.'
The king and queen sang in joy because they're having a baby boy!

Leo Williams (10)
Courtlands Special School, Plymouth

Found My Family

I am at the park,
I am excited,
I am playing in the yellow, soft sand,
I pick the sand up and it feels cold.

My parents are watching me from the wooden bench,
My sisters play nicely on the swings, the swings are big and white,
I turn around and look at the bench.
They are all gone.

I am frightened because I can't see my family,
I run away as fast as a brown rabbit,
I searched for them by the shop,
I run into the shop to buy sweets and chocolates.
It makes me feel a little bit better.

The kind people in the shop help keep me safe.
They shut the doors.
I feel happier because they look after me,
They give me yummy, tasty chocolate and some freezing cold water.

The helpful policeman takes me home in the noisy white police car,
The blue lights are flashing.
I got home and walked into the lounge.
Mummy, Daddy, Jasmine and Jessica were there,
They had waited at home for me.

I was excited to see my family.
I was safe.
I was at home!

Jemma Saundry (10)
Courtlands Special School, Plymouth

The Unicorn

The moon was as bright as a candle,
The stars were twinkling.
The unicorn was as beautiful as a white orchid.
As she landed on the moon,
She knew they needed help soon,
The aliens were about to attack,
The unicorn had to fight back,
Her eyes shot lasers,
But the aliens had tasers.
She needed some back up, so she called her team.
A dog named Bertie and a red panda called Dean.
Bertie and Dean got out their guns,
They started to shoot at the tonnes and tonnes,
Of enemy aliens who were running away.
The unicorn, Bertie and Dean saved the day, hooray!

Leighton Daly (10)
Courtlands Special School, Plymouth

Underwater Adventure

I dived into the water it was as clear as a crystal.
I came across a yellow submarine as bright as the sun
The water felt cold like stepping into a freezer
The submarine jumped towards me.
There was banging on the submarine as loud as thunder
The clowns must be inside
The children were surfing unaware that the clowns were approaching.
In the distance I could see a great white shark.
He came towards me and he struck out his tail.
He hit the submarine which left the water with a *whoosh*.
The clowns were gone forever and the submarine was smashed.

Courtney Hancock (10)
Courtlands Special School, Plymouth

The Spaceship And The Alien

The spaceship smashed into the ground with a massive bang.
The spaceship was sad because it had been ripped into tiny pieces.
The crew escaped the savage wreck.
Then they gazed upon an eerie deck.
The alien stood there with skin as black as coal.
An alien was as frightening as a hungry cheetah.
The alien whooshed past the crew.
He was running as fast as a bullet to make a brew.
The alien stopped and spoke to the crew.
He said, 'Come to my house for a special brew, it's to die for.'
I woke up with a scream
Phew, It was only a dream!

Louis Horne (10)
Courtlands Special School, Plymouth

The Haunted School

The school walls are made from gold and like the sun.
The school windows are big, creepy and covered in cobwebs.
The floorboards started grunting at me.
The chairs bounced as they banged into the tables.
As the chairs banged into the tables they grew with anger.
Suddenly, I could hear the clown's laughing as loud as thunder.
Staring through the creepy window,
The glowing eyes watched.
Then the red fox took the clown to a haunted cave.
When a plane appeared and took us away to Mexico.

Alfie Cox (10)
Courtlands Special School, Plymouth

A Dream About Football

I went to the football pitch.
Ronaldo and Messi came too.
Then we saw Hazard and Dele Alli,
We played with Rooney and Pogba,
Against Benjamin, Jemma and Mr Roberts.
The game had started, the score was 1-1.
Ronaldo scored a goal and it was 2-1.
Then Messi scored.
Then Hazard scored.
Then Dele Alli scored and it was 5-1
Then Benjamin scored to make it 5-2
The whistle blows.
The game is over.
We all said, 'Good game.'
That was a good dream!

Daniel Burt (10)
Courtlands Special School, Plymouth

The Lost Treasures Of The Clown

Once upon a dreamy, but scary time,
We went to an abandoned circus.
Stopping in the soggy, squishy mud, *squish, squash, squish, squash.*
The sky was a black puddle.
Max and his dog looked left and right and he saw a clown,
his face was as white as chalk,
his mouth was as wide as the ocean,
his eyes were burning hot,
It hypnotised the dog,
the dog woke up with eyes redder than blood,
Crying in the cover and I wake up warm and safe in my bed!

Caleb Malloch (10)
Courtlands Special School, Plymouth

Zombie Apocalypse

I was living in an abandoned house,
There was only me.
There is a zombie in the TV.
The TV turns on by itself.

On the screen is the zombie,
Who comes out at me,
The zombie gets closer and closer,
Then a man in an army suit comes in and saves my life.

He takes me to a bunker until the zombie apocalypse is over.
I hear a bell,
I open my eyes, it was a nightmare,
I am safe!

Wei-Heng Beh (11)
Courtlands Special School, Plymouth

A Scary Night

My house was haunted with broken windows,
creepy vampires and zombies were in the cemetery.
The moon was shining bright like a banana.
Birds were gliding like kites.
I was walking down the path splashing in the puddles,
The birds were singing happy tunes like a lady playing the harp.
I turned and I was being followed,
I ran as fast as a motorbike.
Suddenly, I woke up in my bed.
Was it all a dream?

Drew Morshead (9)
Courtlands Special School, Plymouth

Mason Goes To The Circus

I was excited to go to the humongous circus.
The circus was rainbow coloured.
I was excited to see the funny clown.
The clown looked like a purple, yellow and red lollipop.
The lollipop tasted of blueberries, bananas and strawberries.
His red nose is funny and goes *beep! Beep! Beep!*
But that is my alarm clock waking me up.
It's all been a dream!

Mason John Bittle (9)
Courtlands Special School, Plymouth

A Dream

The pug came to the door and said, 'Hi, can I come in?'
He had a glass of coke.
He went to sit on a comfy chair.
He put his coke on the shiny, sparkly, gold table.
Ethan Gamer TV went over to the pug and said,
'Pug, please can I sit next to you?'
Pug said, 'Yes you can sit here because I feel lonely.'
They had a talk about fun things.

Lucas Middleton (11)
Courtlands Special School, Plymouth

A Football Dream

I was in Manchester with Wayne Rooney and Ronaldo.
I came down to Plymouth with them.
To play a game of football at Home Park.
It's very big, it's amazing!
Man Utd and Man City verses Mr Roberts, Plymouth Argyle and Daniel
And Wayne Rooney,
And Ronaldo and Me!
The score is 9-20
Then I went home to Manchester.

Benjamin Richard Seaborne (10)
Courtlands Special School, Plymouth

Stunt Dogs

The crowd went crazy and screamed out loud.
The dogs lined up with their bikes which were talking.
The bikes were laughing out loud, when a dog fell off.
He got back on and waved to the crowd.
They revved the motorbikes and the bikes walked along together.
The dogs used ramps and backflipped like Batman.

Jack Jackson (10)
Courtlands Special School, Plymouth

Spider-Man Dream

Gotham City was scary and spooky,
Spider-Man whooshed down the streets like a gorilla,
Spider-Man asked me to help,
I held on to him as he shot webs onto the buildings,
We swung between the buildings like monkeys
We saved a boy who was lost,
Suddenly I woke up on the floor,
I was happy.

Darran Roberts (10)
Courtlands Special School, Plymouth

Best Dream Ever!

One night I saw my beautiful sister
She was racing a car in space *Whoosh!*
I was diving in slurpy chocolate
And saw a hundred ginormous snakes.
Being eaten by some squishy monsters
I was happy and skipping in there,
With Santa and the elves,
Brushing their grey curly hair.

Ellis MacIntosh (9)
Courtlands Special School, Plymouth

The Fox And The School

The school was hairy and dark like a tarantula covered in cobwebs.
The windows were made of dark crystals.
A fox tried to get me and zoomed past me wearing running shoes.
The fox ran like it was an athlete.
I saw a bunny as fluffy as a teddy.
I felt happy like a cat that purred.

Kian Peart (9)
Courtlands Special School, Plymouth

Ghost Bear

I see a ghost bear
It is as big as the earth,
It is as red as a bus,
I am with my mum,
And my mum is beautiful.

We are in the woods,
And we are very scared,
when the ghost bear chases us,
The ghost bear is super fast,
And then the ghost bear is gone!

Christopher Hallam (9)
Courtlands Special School, Plymouth

Unicorns

Mr and Mrs Unicorn got married.
It's raining fairy dust.
Mr and Mrs Unicorn fly like superheroes down to their world.
The houses talk and sing.
The doorbells go *ping*.

Lola Ann Nutbean (10)
Courtlands Special School, Plymouth

Bunny

The black bunny like the night,
The red bunny likes the apples,
Having a shower in the rain,
Off to the jumpy park.
Jumping on the trampoline,
Boing, boing, boing.

Jasmine Saundry (9)
Courtlands Special School, Plymouth

My Dream

I played with Liverpool at the stadium.
Shouting people,
Eating pasties as big as windows.
Green and red shirts.
George scores a brilliant goal!

George Davies (9)
Courtlands Special School, Plymouth

Mum Is Happy

Mum is happy smiling at home.
My Wii controller is as small as a mouse.
The driving game shouted, 'Well done!'

Flynn Beal (9)
Courtlands Special School, Plymouth

Away With The Fairies

I dream I can fly as high as can be,
And what lovely things my eyes can see.
I'm lost in a jungle swinging on vines,
There's loads of plants, all different kinds.

I dream I'm in London during the blitz,
Bombs smashing things into endless bits.
I'm in the Sahara facing a snake,
Please don't bite me for goodness sake.

I dream I'm swimming in the Barrier Reef
And I wonder what kind of creatures I'll meet.
I'm skydiving out of an aeroplane high,
It was so fast I could barely say bye.

I dream I'm in the city at the dead of night,
The buildings and skyscrapers reaching a great height.
I'm lost in a woodland far, far away,
But then it all vanishes because it's now day.

Daniel Lee (11)
Gotherington Primary School, Cheltenham

It

Last night I had a strange, strange dream,
It even had a strange, strange theme,
About how it came to me,
How it came to be.

Above the world so scruffy,
It whizzed through clouds so puffy,
And looked down on a civilisation,
Descending towards the nation.

The lights of the city bemused
And with no time to have mused,
It dodged between metal trees so tall,
Trying not to fall.

Slowly luscious hills appear,
So there's nothing left to fear,
It spotted something in the distance,
And flying with great persistence.
Found my house in the valley.

That is how it came to be,
Of how it came to me
So next time your wish of sleep comes true,
Think how your dreams get to you.

Kate Coldwell (11)
Gotherington Primary School, Cheltenham

Stuck Fast In Yesterday

A veil of mist curtains me out,
The feeling of terror makes me shout,
The firing of guns is all around,
The blood of men as they fall to the ground,
When will this nightmare end?

Bullets have reached their destination,
Adding to the devastation,
All the rubble and all the fire,
Will the opposition ever tire,
When will this nightmare end?

I can't take it any more,
I'm in a real nightmare I'm sure,
I'm fed up with all this gone,
But this is the Great World War,
When will this nightmare end?

All the lost places,
The forgotten faces,
The sights and sounds go to my head,
But I wake up safe in my own bed,
I think I've found the end!

Freya Lindgren (10)
Gotherington Primary School, Cheltenham

Evil Angels!

Soft, fluffy clouds fill the ground
As I stand there, I hear no sound.
An angry angel flies over me,
It's dress is made from pure white thread,
More and more appear left and right from thin air,
They turn to look at me trembling there,
As the air settles to a silent breeze
The angels divide into threatening threes.
I can hear my heart pounding in fear,
As the angels levitated near,
Suddenly, eyes of red glow upon the faces of the evil angels.
Fear dashes through me like a running athlete.
The evil angels still with glowing red eyes, closing in on me and...
Beep, beep, beep... It's my alarm clock waking me from my sleep!

Lily Marchant (11)
Gotherington Primary School, Cheltenham

One Snowy Dream

When I am deep within my sleep,
Into my mind strange thoughts they creep.
I dream of school on a day that's cool,
And the frost and winter are so cruel.
All my friends are going mad,
to gather the snow that could be had.
I was the queen of the icy throne,
while the teachers stood, cold and alone.
Mr Philcox was stood there,
Though, strangely, he had no hair,
This, my friends and I could not bear,
Mr Jordan was laughing, he fell off his chair.
When my alarm sounded with a beep.
I woke up from an abstract sleep,
Everything was gone, and I was thinking deep
And all I can remember is counting six sheep...

Jesse Elizabeth Steel (9)
Gotherington Primary School, Cheltenham

I See The Sea

I see the sea,
I see the waves washing up on the sand,
I see lots and lots of seashells,
I see children ringing bells,
I see a baby turtle munching on a piece of lettuce.

I see the shining sun,
I see children having fun,
I see people on boats,
I see children with floats.

I see people in huts,
I see people eating nuts,
I see people licking ice creams,
I see children playing on beams.

I see people surfing,
I see people swimming,
I see a shoal of fish,
I see seagulls flying,
I see beagles,
I see the sea.

Amelia Freeman (10)
Gotherington Primary School, Cheltenham

Do You Dream Of...

Do you dream of being a king,
Ruling the world,
Owning some bling?

Do you dream of being a climber,
Or a circus clown,
Balancing on a wire?

Do you dream of driving a car
Winning all the races,
Becoming a star?

Do you dream of being smart,
Inventing new things,
Being there from the start?

Do you dream of being a Dad,
The best in the world,
Wouldn't you be glad?

Do you dream of any of this?
They're not that bad,
They may bring happiness!

Dylan Kingswood (9)
Gotherington Primary School, Cheltenham

A Dreadful Dream

I dreamt a dream, a dreadful dream,
One very stormy night,
It gave me quite a fright.

I was in Unicorn Land,
My very own world,
Where everyone was happy,
Then it all turned.

There were fights and there was war.
But then it all came to me,
Once a year it all turns around,
And infects all the magical beasts.

They all turn bad,
All naughty and boisterous and sad
That is why Unicorn Land is banished
To the land of all dreadful dreams.

Katie Marsh (10)
Gotherington Primary School, Cheltenham

I Will Believe!

My friends say I should not believe in things that cannot be true.
But my heart one must exist as real as me or you.
So I don't listen to those who swear,
That things they cannot see aren't there.
I am a unicorn, free and wild.
And someday I will find a child.

Huw Evans (10)
Gotherington Primary School, Cheltenham

Dead Forever Inside

Deep inside my heart is gone,
Nowhere to be found.
Everywhere I go something is a problem.
A shadow I see is as scary as it will be.
Dark in my heart is somewhere to be found.
Faith in my heart but nowhere to be seen.
Oh my heart where will you lead me to life or death help me.
Relieve me from dark, but to see you cry.
Every death I take is taking me nowhere.
Very old but, what I see is red, nothing else.
Every step I take leads to life, sometimes to death.
Really poor, I starve all night which makes me dead more.
In my heart something is coming this way,
Night is bright but my heart is as dark,
Stars like my heart but the dark one in one life my heart is blue then the day after.
I hope my life continues every year I'm happy and joyful and full of happiness.

Manfoosah Maria Begum (7)
Sheringham Primary School, London

Dancing In Your Dream

D ancing on stage, dancing together having fun on a bright, beautiful day.
A nything you want, everything you think can always come true if you try.
N atural day, great year, time for a new year!
C an you dream? Can you dance? Of course you can because you have potential
I n your dream you dream something new always happens, whether good or bad you can always have a good
N ight or day, you can always follow your dream
G oodbye, hope you had a good day, no one can take your dreams.

Nene Isatou Jallow (8)
Sheringham Primary School, London

Mr Dragon

Come back my dragon
I couldn't see you last night
I waded through angry clouds to find your tail and they gave me quite a fright.
Your eyes are shiny and the night is dark.
Its silence is deep.
I want to talk to you.
Just before I sleep.
It will bring me peace.
It will make me smile, hearing your voice,
Making life worthwhile
Fly dragon, fly, higher and higher.
Breathe dragon, breathe,
Blink dragon blink,
Your eyes of gold.
Sleep dragon sleep,
You are ever so old.

Ashir Imran (8)
Sheringham Primary School, London

My Imagination

I am in my imagination
M y friends are with me
A ll the things in my imagination are things that I can see
G oodness me, I'm amazed to see
I can see all the things that I imagine.
N o one is here except me and my friends
A re all these things real?
T oday is the day I saw my imagination for real
I have seen everything
O h, it's a dream come true
N ow it's possible to see my imagination.

Madeeha Rahman (8)
Sheringham Primary School, London

Friendship

F riends are all you need
R ight there next to you is where they seek
I f you go through a hard time they will be there
E ntertaining you is their job
N ever will they ever hurt you
D oing what's good for you
S tanding up for you no matter what
H elping you wherever you are
I t's what friends are for
P romise they'll always be there for you.

Iqra Miah (7)
Sheringham Primary School, London

The Sprinkles Of Luck! The Sprinkles Of Wisdom!

S prinkles oh sprinkles
P erhaps very lucky
R ight kind of sprinkles for me
I 've never had sprinkles as lucky as you
N ow your so lucky, let's see the future for you
K endle's coming to examine you, how do you feel?
L ately you've given me ideas
E ven Kendle gets ideas from you
S prinkles oh sprinkles help us please.

Leeana Tahiyyah (8)
Sheringham Primary School, London

Unicorns

U nicorns, unicorns such lovely creatures
N ow I feel safe with you beautiful unicorn
I 'm a unicorn oh, so friendly
C ome back Mr Unicorn please, may I stroke you?
O h you're a lovely unicorn let's play a game
R oyal unicorns are the fairest of them all
N ow I feel safe with you Mr Unicorn
S o many lovely unicorns.

Afifa Nuzha (8)
Sheringham Primary School, London

Harry Potter

H arry Potter, I wish I was you
A nd knew magic
R onald Weasley
R eally, you're so funny
Y es! Time to dream!

P otter!
O h no! I forgot my cauldron
T he worst person in the class!
T he worst person in the class?
E ars hear this
R eally, he's the best!

Hamdaan Hussain (7)
Sheringham Primary School, London

My Funny Poem

When I smile I run a mile.
I dial my friend to see if he can bend.
I watch a movie but soon it ends.
Did I ever tell you my dad can lend, but he does not share
One day, I did go to the fair,
But my friend just didn't seem to care.
And then I saw a dream flying in the air.
I tried to catch it, but it just kept on disappearing.

Enos Eyassu (8)
Sheringham Primary School, London

Fairies

F airies in the dark
A t night, creeping through the forest
I nteresting sounds in the dark
R ainy days, fairies in mini shelters
I ts wings shining in the dark
E very day flying around the world
S neaking around the world looking at people.

Ajwah Qasim (7)
Sheringham Primary School, London

Rainbow Land

I dream and see things that include me
By aiming high and to be successful is the key.
I have gone to places where no one has ever been.
As exciting as it is in reality and in my dream.
Amazing as it is so colourful and bright,
It's the end of the rainbow that does me right.

Jay Singh Sommers (7)
Sheringham Primary School, London

Dream

D ream is a wish that always lives in my heart
R ound the clock twenty-four hours
E nergise me to run after it without being tired
A brave girl, defeat the fear inside the dark and a shining sun came out
M y world is safe, and my dreams comes true.

Meerab Fouz Butt (8)
Sheringham Primary School, London

Wild Dream Land

In Dreamland, everyone walks on their heads, like an elegant acrobat.
This is what goes on in my wild Dreamland.
In Dreamland, all the boys wear dresses as bright as the sun.
This is what goes on in my wild Dreamland.
In Dreamland, the children are the teachers, and the adults are the pupils.
This is what goes on in my wild Dreamland.
In Dreamland, the floor makes a bouncing sound, and when you jump on it, you go as high as an angel dancing in the sky.
In Dreamland, all the people growl like an animal, and the animals chatter like humans.
This is what goes on in my wild Dreamland.
I wish that I could stay some more, but when my shocking alarm starts to squawk, I have to say, 'Goodbye Dreamland'.

Aurelia Westlake (8)
St Anthony's School For Girls, London

Weird World

In Dreamland round roses riddle you,
Rodents run wild round your feet,
Bees bumble and bounce.
Flowers flutter on the roaring wind.

The sky is swathed in blue,
You can flit and fly like a swallow in summer,
Forests are full of animals.
All the tree trunks bend and bow so, you can climb.

The sun shines all day,
And the wind whistles a cool tune.
And when it snows it feels warm,
The best time is spring, but all of it is great.

Summer is leaf green parrots,
Autumn in round, red robins
Winter is swooping snowy owls
I'm always sad to bid farewell but I can't help waking up.

Romilly Burgess (7)
St Anthony's School For Girls, London

A Unicorn Dream

Once I had a dream I turned into a unicorn
Pretty looking unicorns flying all around
The sky was like pretty and pink cotton candy clouds, we ate all day long
Pretty looking unicorns flying all around
We flew, *whoosh, whoosh, whoosh*, like an eagle past the clouds
Pretty looking unicorns flying all around
We soared faster than a space rocket headed for the moon
Pretty looking unicorns flying all around
Soon my mum will wake me up,
so goodbye every unicorn, goodbye, goodbye, goodbye!
Pretty looking unicorns flying all around.

Helena Mayo (8)
St Anthony's School For Girls, London

Candy Land

In Dreamland, the clouds are fairy floss that smell like flowers.
Horses and squirrels are pets like cats and dogs.
Plants and trees smell like perfume.
Bubble gum that's a bubbly like liquid.
In Dreamland at school they have candy that whiffs of chicken.
The wind shouts like a baby screaming.

Lollipops waltz on chocolate mountains in Dreamland.
You have a jelly bean for a roof.
Everyone in Dreamland is blissful.

And your house is made from gingerbread.
I don't want to wake up!

Macy Lehmann (7)
St Anthony's School For Girls, London

The Best Dream Ever

You have no school, no work, no homework.
Everyone's so happy in Dreamland.

Cotton Candy Clouds are so puffy and so soft.
Everyone's so happy in Dreamland.

Everybody can fly and you do what you want. Eat junk food!
Everyone's so happy in Dreamland.

People's mouths water when they see the yummy chocolate chip trees.
Everyone's so happy in Dreamland.

Unicorns and squirrels make good pets.
Everyone's so happy in Dreamland.

Irem Cenkci (7)
St Anthony's School For Girls, London

Midnight Dream

In Dreamland, the sky howls like a dangerous wolf and is as black as shiny boots.
It's upside down in Dreamland,

Everyone is frightened as the wind sings a melancholy melody.

It's upside down in Dreamland.

Wild animals chatter violently like naughty children

It's upside down in Dreamland

Luckily, I can escape because my mum is calling, so I wake.

It's upside down in Dreamland.

Ellie Davidson (7)
St Anthony's School For Girls, London

My Wonderful Dream

It's splendid in Dreamland,
The emerald grass is made out of jelly beans,
You can wish whatever you like,
The sky is as pink as cotton candy,
There's no school so you can eat sweets and play tricks,
People skip in Dreamland so everyone is joyful like they slurped ice cream.
Months whiz by in the blink of an eye as time speeds by.
Unfortunately, I have to go but don't worry I'll come tomorrow,
When I tiptoe to my cosy bed.

Carlotta Bruno (8)
St Anthony's School For Girls, London

Living In The Clouds

Way up high in the sky,
Is where my Dreamland is,
It's filled with clouds and lots of pie,
and time goes by in a whiz.

But when you enter my Dreamland dear,
many rainbows you will see,
followed by magical unicorns coming near,
with me riding them, Whoopee!

Let's not forget about my phone,
With YouTube, music and games,
when I have my phone I'll never moan,
Even if it rains!

When you turn and look around,
A swimming pool you will see,
But then to my surprise I would've found
A Jacuzzi just for me!

That's when you start to wonder,
What's the atmosphere like?
There's definitely no rain or thunder,
Only bright and happy colours that are hard to dislike!

The vibe is as happy as a unicorn,
The grass as soft as fur
Trees that grow sweets, so fun,
And sweet, fluffy cats that purr.

When I wake up in the morning,
I open my eyes and look around in the bright,
No cats or unicorns or music playing,
That's when I said, 'I'll just go back tonight.'

Meagan Jade Sanchez (11)
St Edward's Catholic Primary School, London

The Life Of Dance

In the life of dance we have a very big vision,
Where we try our best to make a good impression.
We dance with might and all our hearts,
We try to get up when our confidence falls apart.
Twirling on stage, being courageous,
Keeping our balance all night, so outrageous!
The world of dance, just begun, sounds quite tiring, but it's actually fun.
Dance for me, is life's new trend, as everyone is part of it, for example my friends.
Dance is the world's chain and harmony, we work together to create a cool fantasy.
Keeping your posture, making yourself proud, dancing your own solo, in front of a crowd.
In dance, the main key is resilience and love, get ready for coming challenges down or above.
Stay strong in any dancing leap as dance is a fantasy that we should keep!

Jayla Jayne Jara (10)
St Edward's Catholic Primary School, London

Showstopper

Taking a picture before we go on,
humming and whistling to our new song.
Getting quite nervous, just hearing the crowd,
Screaming and shouting they sure are loud!
'Everyone get ready for Melanie and Jackie.'
I was so nervous while Jackie looked happy!
The crowd's going wilder just hearing our names!
'This was always my dream having fame.'
Next thing you know I'm on stage with my friend.
Singing in harmony, the fun will never end.
A few minutes later, the show was over.
I felt as lucky as a four leaf clover.
But after the performance we got a surprise
I was so shocked I couldn't believe my eyes.
It was Sophia Grace!
Suddenly I woke up, it was all a dream.
It was an absolute show stopper!

Melanie Alphonse (10)
St Edward's Catholic Primary School, London

I Wish I Came Back

I'm sitting in the corner alone,
Crying, I miss my old school and home,
Will I go back to Spain?
Or will I be in pain?

I lost everything that I loved,
My house, my feelings and everything above,
The days will not be the same,
Without the sun, the wind and so much rain.

I miss my family,
Grandpas, cousins and those beloved eternally,
I loved the weather,
It was comforting like a feather.
Everyone is so friendly,
And I don't ever feel lonely,
We try to be helpful,
And mostly are grateful.

London is my new home,
Where my new friends and I will roam.

Genoveva Martin (10)
St Edward's Catholic Primary School, London

The Fears Of A Deep Sleep

N ight falls upon the world and I suddenly drift off to sleep.
I woke up in this strange world and wondering where I ought to be
G as coming out from the piece of land I see, I suddenly take a gigantic leap
H umans in the distance I think I see
T he smoke behind me seems to becoming nearer
M y eyes are out of focus as the humans in front of me become less and less cleaner
A ll of the smoke covers my way and stops me in my tracks
R un, run, get out before it's too late, I heard a voice say
E verything around me turned black and I suddenly woke up and it's day.

Chelsea Angeles (10)
St Edward's Catholic Primary School, London

Fairy Dream

Here I come, welcomed to bed lying there with my teddy, Ted.
Sleeping in bed, feeling all right inside my bed, snuggling up tight.
Feeling a tingle, ready for a dream.
Here I come, but seeing some steam walking through, in a sight of smoke.
So confused, left with a soak.
Travelling through, relieving a star
Ambling through, catch a sight of sparks afar running through, seeing a bright spark transforming into something.
Oh look! A fantastic fairy!
Looks nice! But never scary, feeling so surprised.
But I wake up.
Yawning on a different date knowing it was all a dream...

Kassandra Mae Delos Reyes (9)
St Edward's Catholic Primary School, London

Look, Look! A Dinosaur

Look, look! A dinosaur,
It's green! Well it's enormous,
It stomped and roared
But it's nameless.

I could name it Burgery,
No, how about big roaring Lee?
I was so distracted that he was able to flee
I thought he was able to flee because of me.

I looked around but I couldn't see him,
I soon realised it was starting to look dim,
Then came a big bang,
Soon followed by a slam.

Then I felt a sunbeam,
Making me think it was a dream,
Little do I know that it was real,
Which made my banana peel.

Paul Manzon (10)
St Edward's Catholic Primary School, London

Dancers Always Try

D o your best and be yourself!
A lways follow the steps and rhythm
N ever give up on dancing!
C an learn a routine
E asy or hard, but try!
R emember the steps
S ee and listen to the movements.

A dancer never gives up that easy/quick!
L earn a step
W e make new friends
A lways listen!
Y ou should never give up on anything!
S o never stop trying!

T o make new friends
R emember to not fuss
Y ou do your best.

Divine Okua (8)
St Edward's Catholic Primary School, London

Farewell To My Dear Friend

In this solitary night, I am awake thinking of you.
It is raining and cold outside.
But my heart is burning like a fire in a chimney.
In all the beautiful memories, that we cherished our friendship.
I weep silently in my dreams.
You are not with me to wipe off my tears.
You are far away...we laughed, we screamed, we fought and cried.
But Lavender fragrance symbolised our friendship.
It hurts me every moment.
Your absence is going to leave an empty space in my soul...
I miss you...
My life will be priceless without your blossoming smile...

Tessa Agnes Arun (10)
St Edward's Catholic Primary School, London

In A Fox's Dream

Nothing I see, nothing I say.
Little fox doesn't even say, 'Hey!'
It's a rainy, stormy night.
You might get a fright.

Walking through the meadows what do I see?
A white tall skeleton looking at me.
The skeleton grabs me
As cold as I can be.

Oh no, the skeleton is taking me to a haunted house
I don't want a scary little pet mouse.
The scary skeleton guards me but soon falls asleep.
I find out he is a robot, that falls asleep in seconds, how cheap.
Quietly I go
Going super slow.

Ozi Daisy-Divine Oparaugo (8)
St Edward's Catholic Primary School, London

The Mouse And The Bee Who Caused Such Commotion

A woman who once heard a mouse,
ran screaming throughout her house,
here and there,
that she could not bear,
then entered a little bee.
The poor old woman expeditiously fled.

The house was filled with tumultuous noise,
causing neighbours eardrums to be destroyed,
who knew such small animals could make such a fuss,
the whole neighbourhood took a bus to get away from the squeak and buzz,
I woke up and found my mum yelling at me, hold on...
This was all a prodigious dream!

Angel Nana Achiaa Asamoah (11)
St Edward's Catholic Primary School, London

My World

Delicate wishes all around,
Glistening gently without a sound,
A world just for me.

Air flows quietly, carelessly,
Dancing with the leaves, gracefully,
A world, beautiful as can be.

Strong and fragrant stunning roses,
I walk ahead, the gate closes,
In my world full of glee!

The sun begins to rise, the fun doesn't last
I'll remember this always, future, present or past.
A world where I am truly happy!

Chienyemona Wright (11)
St Edward's Catholic Primary School, London

Dream Imagination

Roses are red, the sky is blue,
Where does your imagination take you?

Where am I? Am I home? Or in Sandy's tree dome.
Am I small? or just too tall?

I'm in the park, in the dark?
Then a bear is sitting in a chair in its lair
having a cup of tea and getting a book to read.

I end up in school, now in a pool
Then to bed where I calmly said,
'It was a dream, oh well, I need to get ready for show and tell.'

Nayara Simoes (9)
St Edward's Catholic Primary School, London

Superpower

S upernatural humans are taking the world
U nity is my sidekick his
P owers are teleportation
E lectro dynamite is a mortal enemy
R ay is my name, my powers are vision
P rotection is our duty
O ur powers can save the
W orld
E verything must count to save innocent people
R emember
S ee you when the war ends.

Darren Guba (10)
St Edward's Catholic Primary School, London

Fly High Up In The Sky

One day I was in my room gazing out at a plane.
I imagined I could fly so high up in the sky and spread my wings.
I saw a bird flying high flapping its wings and flying freely.
Fly, fly up high like a bird in the sky.

Olivia Nkili Molokwu (10)
St Edward's Catholic Primary School, London

Flying

F reezing cold up in the sky
L ying between the clouds
Y ellow sun can be seen
I n the metal bird
N o problems up in the sky
G ravity is not required.

Ezekiel Clement (9)
St Edward's Catholic Primary School, London

Pokémon Poem

This is my Pokémon Poem, you all should know,
Just sit down and read this, you're in for a show!
We start with the Pokémon Bulbasaur,
His name reminds me of a Carnataur,
Then there's Charmander who is sweet and cute,
He's even more cuter in a playsuit!
Also comes the tiny turtle Squirtle,
He's very good at jumping over a hurdle!
Then there's the great Venusaur,
Maybe his ancestor is a dinosaur!
The incredible Charizard who's fire-flying,
Also does lots of crying!
The awesome water type is Blastoise,
Who has the weight of a tortoise!
The incredible legendary Rayquaza flies high,
Spots Groudon and Kyogre is he a spy?
The legendary ice Pokémon Kyurem is quite a breeze,
He even might give you a sneeze!
All the Pokémon are amazing and spectacular
Whoever created them, I'm quite peculiar.

Phillip Wayne Torres (9)
St Mary's RC Primary School, London

My Worst Nightmare...

Finally I get into my bed,
On my pillow I rest my head.
I enter a different world when I dream
Where things are never as they seem.

In my dream, I... picture myself standing in the middle of Kensington Palace
All of a sudden, I'm handed a golden chalice.
I drink it all up in one big gulp,
Then without warning I have the hiccups.

In one quick flash the luxury is gone,
and in front of me are zombies who weigh at least a tonne.
There's zombies here and zombies there
And in the corner - there's zombies everywhere!
But here and there you might see...

Some skeletons and vampires looking at me.
I take a step forward as nervous as can be.
Glancing left and right,
All I see is smoke,
How did I get here?
I hope this is a joke

Thud! Something moved
It's creeping me around.
My worst nightmare is realised...

Nevaeh Harris (11)
St Mary's RC Primary School, London

The Man Who Saw Everything!

The man wearing a cape,
saw an ape,
eating a grape.

The man was talking to his mate
and realised he was late
for his special debate.

There was a boy
who had a toy
and his name was Troy.

He saw his teacher
and he stared at her as if she was a creature
that taught a double feature.

He sat on his chair
and said a little prayer
after he saw a bear.

He started to get lost
and he passed some frost
he checked how much it cost to defrost.

He looked on the floor
It had the number four
then he looked at what he wore.

The woman went in her house
wearing a blouse
printed with a mouse.

He opened the door
he had to do a chore
then he wanted more.

He saw me
What did he see?
He saw a girl holding a key!

Charmelle Eligado (9)
St Mary's RC Primary School, London

Sweet Vs Sour

Once upon a time in my dream,
I got lost and I really screamed.
Screamed like a baby till I found,
Pancake land which was all mine.
Sweet, delicious, golden liquid
swirling all around.
Strawberries, rosy as a child's cheeks
jumping and laughing about.
Happy, jolly land, 'Oh dear I love you so much,'
till a pickle knight comes along and tries to destroy us.
Attacked the sweetness of heaven
this unruly sour taste.
What the world will begin,
if they may win their case?
I'm tossing, turning, swirling mad,
I don't know what to do!
Oh Mother dear please come
and don't let my dream come true!
The pickle king dies smothered in jelly
because he landed in a child's belly.
Now I can continue with my dream

sweet sugar rush come to me.
No pickles, no wars, no funny taste
I never want anything sour in my face.

Dorien Ortutai-Hughes (7)
St Mary's RC Primary School, London

Night Sky

Let no one keep you down
You should never have a frown
Your limit is the sky
If you believe you can fly.

The night sky is blue
That doesn't mean you have to be too.
You could sit next to the king of the sky
And daze upon the stars in your kingly throne
When you're in the sky, anywhere is your home.

Jump into bed and dream away
Rule your kingdom in the clouds
Or go somewhere and be really loud.

You could go beyond your wildest dreams
Even beyond this world
When your happy, nothing can stop you.

When you're dreaming, you could be a pirate with your crew.
Just remember,
Nothing can stop you.
When you're down.
Remember the night sky is blue.
That doesn't mean you have to be too.

Sean George Murphy (10)
St Mary's RC Primary School, London

Candy Land

Chocolate butterflies
Candy trees
Swirly lollipops
Fudge bunnies.

This is land where the candy queen lives
Her hair, her eyes are covered in whip.
Whip cream, whip ice
That's everything so,
but this is my dream where the candy queen goes.

Next are her servants
The ones who shall serve.
They're strong and mighty, as fearsome as her.

The candy cars well I think you might know.
They drove around town didn't you know,
Some small, some big, some tiny ones too,
but you should be careful they're smaller than you!

This is my story about one candy land.
The candy queen reigns the Oreos band.
It's so very wild,
It's so very mad,
So why not come join us in Candy Land.

Chloe Jessica Cummins (10)
St Mary's RC Primary School, London

Dinosaurs

I went to my favourite place
Somewhere I've always wanted to go
A place full with dinosaurs called Jurassic Park
I hid down very low.

I walked across a pond and got wet
I'd ruined my new trousers - I was upset!
I sat on the grass to have a break
Next thing you know, I had a tummy ache.

Behind me stood a large dinosaur
With humongous horns
The triceratops sat next to a bunch of acorns.

An alarm sounded that was like a nuke was inbound.
But it meant the most dangerous dinosaur was around.

The triceratops crushed the dangerous T-rex like a pin
Then you'll never guess - he ate him!

I woke up with a fright
It was hard to go back to sleep that night.

David Waldoch (10)
St Mary's RC Primary School, London

Last Night's Dream

Last night's dream
I thought that it was true,
I wondered what's inside of it
so out the door I went through...

All I saw was a very bright
light that started to blind me,
but as the place became darker
a huge crowd I see.

I realised I was on stage
and in the centre was a mic.
They told me to sing for them,
sing to them all night.

It was an amazing experience
to do what I love most,
If only I could stay with them
and sing with them, I hope.

Every time I sing, I see myself in a
place where I can truly be myself,
Whatever song I choose,
Whatever note I play,
music will always save the day.

Jerrimae De Vera (10)
St Mary's RC Primary School, London

Fantasy World

Every time I close my eyes, an adventure awaits me.
I smile as I fall asleep,
who knows what I will see?

When I'm in the world, I swim with the mermaids in the beautiful deep blue sea.
The fairies give me fairy dust so they can fly with me.
I do some magic tricks with the wizard and I huddle with the bear during storms and blizzards.

I suddenly jump when I meet a talking tree.
As it tells me about its life. I think how can this be?
I'm greeted by a friendly unicorn.
From its head sticks a bright purple horn.
Fairies dance around my head.
I smile as I cuddle up inside my bed.

Keira Dugasse (10)
St Mary's RC Primary School, London

My Teddy Bear

He has a cape I call him Timmy,
but he calls himself Super Teddy.

I wish.
That he would have the power:
To make pizza.
I wish that he had a Lamborghini that was black and yellow.
I wish that he would have a bat cave.

I dream.
That he could fly or glide or shoot a star down from the sky.
I dreamt he had a chicken sword that he used when he's bored.

What does he do in my bed.
Waiting, waiting, waiting for a hug.
Coming in the house I say sweet home, sweet home.
Coming on my bed a frowning face he does.
I give him a hug.
What a smile he does.

Joshua De Sousa (11)
St Mary's RC Primary School, London

Walking Around

From my memory, I was in a large land
Full of vibrance and joy.
Around me was nature, nothing was bland
I looked at myself, just a little boy.

Looking at the trees, as high as I could see
The animals eating merrily, then darting around.
I wandered around, jumping so free.
I heard the surrounding animals, which made a mean sound.

By myself, I walked far away.
To a calm and silent beach, where the waves of the sea swirled.
I had so much fun, it was an eventful day,
But I soon vanished from the world.
And I was in my comfortable bed,
With no dreams in my head.

Lawrence Pascua (10)
St Mary's RC Primary School, London

Bridge Difference

Finally I get into bed
On my pillow, I rest my head
I enter a different world when I dream.

In my dream, I see a massive blue chrome bridge
Strangely in the centre, stands a black metallic fridge,
inside hides famous You Tubers and footballers.
It even contains a flying astronaut with super duper powers.

I now feel really weird and dizzy because Ronaldo just made me a drink that was fizzy!
Suddenly, the drink makes me really tall, I've left and standing in a mall.
Out of nowhere a dinosaur stomps into action.
And at Nat West he makes a low transaction.

Euan Castillo (10)
St Mary's RC Primary School, London

When I Close My Eyes

I close my eyes...
I'm in a place where stars shine bright.
The moon is bigger than my house and lighting up the night.
I walk for miles...
Until I see a beautiful fairy sitting on a mushroom,
Smiling with glee.
Her hair is as blue as the deep sea.
Her wings are painted colours from the galaxy.

She looked at me with a twinkle in her eye and said,
'Would you like to fly?'
Grabbing my hand, we flew up high, higher and higher
In the starry night sky...

I open my eyes...
I'm back in my bed...
Why did we have to stop?...

Ashley Oliveira Pereira Da Silva (11)
St Mary's RC Primary School, London

Nightmares

N othing is always as they seem in my dreams
I close my eyes, take a think, my head exploring dreamworld
G etting my head together, looking left and right
H owever, all I see is darkness
T he atmosphere becomes more crowded as I move closer
M y worst fear is finding myself in a nightmare
A hand grabs my toes as it feels like a creature not from this world
R unning with fear, toys start crawling towards me
E yes start blinking constantly, I close my own in dread
S uddenly I wake up to find myself at home in bed.

Christina Panisales (11)
St Mary's RC Primary School, London

Worst Job In The Entire World

I thought that being a teacher would be the best job!
But it's not because of a man named Bob.

This is the worst job ever!
However, some pupils listen and are so clever.
I should've never picked this job, like never!

There's a teacher who is called Mr Lazybugs
And no one understands why he brings so many rugs!

I walked into a classroom and expected a bloom,
instead I saw a witch with a broom!

I feel so stressed, I don't know what to do?
One of my students asked, 'What, when, where, who?'

Wintana Dawit (10)
St Mary's RC Primary School, London

Posh Unicorn In Space With Servant Pug

Finally I get into bed
Enchanting images float around my head
I snuggle under the blankets tight
Where will my dreams take me tonight?

Overhead I see lots of stars
As I stand on Planet Jupiter
Turning around, what do I see?
A vibrant unicorn standing behind me
It wasn't alone - oh no sir!
A beautiful pug stood beside her.

The unicorns eyes sparkled like a queen
Next thing you know, she threw the pug to me!

Now I have a pug, I forget the rest
When I dream, it truly is the best!

Freya-Lee O'Dea (11)
St Mary's RC Primary School, London

The Unicorn Hair Is Ruined!

Stella was taking a shower
But there seems to be someone looking,
Someone... from Twinkle Town
Looking and searching.

It seems to be some trouble
There seems to be some mystery.
And until Ace will confess
There's trouble can't you see?

Well, you see, Ace dyed someone's hair.
And it was done by Ace.
He dyed Queen Stella's hair
So now, show your face.

But most of all, Queen Stella's pastel rainbow hair was...
All a murky, muddy brown colour!

Hanneka Cabantes (10)
St Mary's RC Primary School, London

Wildest Dream About Unicorns!

A unicorn
As you smell like popcorn
As you make my day
from the darkest colour grey.

As I look for you in the night
your powers shine so bright
As you dance on rainbows
You wear your colourful bows.

Your bright rainbow tail
Was as swirly as a snail
Take me to a scene
When you are the colour of my dreams.

As I hear you really well
with a shining bell
Before I go to bed
I need to write something with my lead
That's why I love unicorns!

Jazmine Ali (10)
St Mary's RC Primary School, London

Dreams!

Dreams can be funny, they can be sad.
They can be happy maybe a bit mad
As I descend into a faraway land
Every new day my dream will expand.

As I shut my eyes
I was awaited with a surprise
You can put away the occupied day
It doesn't matter what price to pay.

Each new day is a new adventure
A great world I will enter
Dreams can be anything you want them to be
A brand new world I will enter.

I wish I could fly
I will fly high into the sky.

Marcel Jnolewis (10)
St Mary's RC Primary School, London

Dreams Come True

Dreams come true and I will tell how.
Ever since I was a baby,
All I think about is a majestic holiday on an island.
Dreams come true and I will tell you how.
A beautiful island with hotels to die for,
Sand as yellow as the sun and a beautiful sapphire ocean.

Dreams come true and I will tell you how to tell you believe in yourself
and magical thing will appear
Dreams come true and I have just told you why a majestic area where you will like.
Dreams come true.

Daisy Gonzalez (11)
St Mary's RC Primary School, London

In Candyland

I'm lost in Candyland
But then the princess takes my hand.

We became best friends
Our friendship will never end.

Candyfloss trees and sugar bees
Those are all the things that we can see.

Then we walk and find a pond
And we spotted a few swans.

But now in my bed, I stand and stare.
All I know is that dream wasn't bare.

That dream was great
But now I'm awake.

Carlee-Jane Senorin (8)
St Mary's RC Primary School, London

Last Night I Dreamt About Pugs

Last night I dreamt about pugs
They were everywhere
They were on my bed
They were sleeping on my chest.
They were small and some were big.
But especially they were jumping on the bed.
All I can see is pugs, pugs, pugs.

They were on my tables
They were on my chair and they were on my hair.
They barked at the door.
They were barking all night long.
But they were strange.
But they drove me barking mad!

Adriana Da Silva (11)
St Mary's RC Primary School, London

The Dream About Unicorns

Last night I dreamed about unicorns
They were everywhere.
There were small ones and big ones.
To bland ones and bright ones too.
The dream about unicorns were amazingly special to me,
because I am a fan of unicorns.
A dream about unicorns is awesome because it is like winter.
Unicorns twist but, don't be mistaken.
They are real in dreams.
Anything can come true...

Megan Ellen Conway-Faulds (11)
St Mary's RC Primary School, London

Happy Thoughts

Back and forth
Up and down.
Faster and faster.
Until I jump on the ground.

Round and round
My head is feeling dizzy
Feeling faint
I need something cold and fizzy.

To the top
We rush to go
To the end
We speedily flow.

Oh no!
It was just a dream
At least after school
I'll know where to flee.

Shanola Toussaint-Soaga (10)
St Mary's RC Primary School, London

Insomnia

I nsomnia, what a disease
N ight remedy balm come help me please!
S ilence breeds through the room
O h Mum! 'Will it be morning soon?'
M um cries, 'Just go to sleep!'
N ever will I have a sleep so deep
I toss and turn, 'Why is the night sky so black?!'
A nxiously I lie and feel like an insomniac.

Gina Paiva Godinho (10)
St Mary's RC Primary School, London

The Nightmare

Where am I? What is this place?
There are no lights, lamps or windows.
I take a step forward, my hairs stand up on my neck.
Then I realised there's someone standing there,
Then he laughs, I ran like I was an Olympic sprinter.
It is colder and the maniac touches me on the shoulder...
Then suddenly, I wake up and I'm in the safety of my own bed.

Cameron Williams (11)
St Mary's RC Primary School, London

The Dream About Tigers

Last night I dreamed
about tigers.
There were tigers everywhere
They were on my head,
They were sleeping on my bed.
They were fighting me,
punching me and they were cuddling me.

They were on my tables,
On my chairs,
On my chandeliers and on my hair.
There were tigers, tigers, tigers.

Jazmin O'Brien (10)
St Mary's RC Primary School, London

I Had A Dream

I had a dream,
where everywhere
was filled with
happiness and loneliness.

I had a dream.
It started sad,
but, ended happy.

I had a dream,
where a dream
can be sad,
a dream can be mad,
a dream can be happy,
a dream can be slappy.

Savannah Martin-Lansiquot (11)
St Mary's RC Primary School, London

Fairy Land

I am in Fairy Land
Flying high,
touching the sky.
Enjoying the ride.

I look down,
and see the grass.
It's green and wet.
And looks so nice.

I come down inside to be sick
The fairies by my side.

Layla Harris (7)
St Mary's RC Primary School, London

Lying Down To Sleep

I dream...
I see them running
Wild and free
In the fields
Wild and free
Is where they love to be.

Strong, powerful, majestic and sleek
Is how they are to me.
Horses, wild and free.

Skye Harris (10)
St Mary's RC Primary School, London

Nightmare, Nightmare!

During the whole daytime,
I'm happy, happy, happy.
But, when the sun comes down and the moon comes up.
It's night, when I'm in my bed and when everyone is in a deep sleep.
Dreaming off to Wonderland.
That's when I get scared.

The only sound I can hear, is my dad's loud snoring.
Which often gets boring,
I can even hear the tweeting of the owl outside.
And I can hear the wind howling like a wolf (how this wind blows oh heaven knows)
And that's when my imagination starts.

I think of a hairy, scary clown!
With a big, round and fat belly,
And with a pointy nose just like Pinocchio,
and whenever, he climbs each step to my bedroom.
His nose gets longer and longer.
Until he reached my bedroom door he stopped.
At that moment at that second at that hour.
My mum came into my room.
And said brightly, 'It's time to get ready to go to school.'

Heba Bouzerar (9)
St Matthias CE Primary School, London

The Athlete Runs For Her Life!

As I walk down the track and my friends say, 'Hi.'
But where am I?
The fog is in my face and it feels like I'm in space!
I take a deep breath and have a little rest after all the work I have done.
Suddenly something's behind me.
I can't really see.
But I can see just me,
I carry on walking but, then I see a monster, it's after me.
I say, 'Who is it?'
But they ignore me!
I run for my life,
I take one more deep breath.
Then I wake up and it was all just a nightmare.
I go downstairs say, 'Good morning, have a cup of tea.'
And wipe the tears and say, 'I have you, don't leave me and always be with me!'

Tayler Campbelle Clarck (10)
St Matthias CE Primary School, London

The Nightmare

I go to my bed ready to dream of magnificent stuff!
I close my eyes... fall asleep
Hold on. Why is this dark?
I try to look for light, no luck.
What was that noise?
The shadows walk in, following more.
Holy Moly! A psycho murderer!
Come on wake up!
But he greets me? Suspicious.
He takes me to his house, scary...
He puts me on a rope. He trapped me?
Ah come on. Get out!
No use, he's coming closer with a big knife!
Ouch! He marks my arm
Wait, no not the *ch-aaah!*
I wake up, breathing fast, Phew! Just a nightmare,
Let's go back to sleep!

Lorenzo Perzhilla (9)
St Matthias CE Primary School, London

John Cywing And Khai Power!

John and Khai came straight out the hood
With their antics and people trying to stop them but no one could.

Whoop! Whoop! That's the sound of the police.
John and Khai were tired and wanted some peace.

The police kept coming
So John and Khai started running.

They were running as fast as they could
Now the police knew they were no good.

Now they were flying
Also the police engine was frying.

John and Khai hid in a shop
The police couldn't find them so they had to stop.

Khaiden Kentebe (10)
St Matthias CE Primary School, London

Sinking

I looked around me
Everything was silent even though I was surrounded by screams.
The waves pushed against my ice-cold body, like hard, sharp knives.
I held my breath as the water slowly rose above my head.
Slowly but surely I started finding it was hard to breathe.
I was so overwhelmed.
I was so scared.
My body froze like a bunch of snow.
On one side of the sea was just the sea.
On the other side wasn't just me there were lots of people including me.

Tilly Latham (9)
St Matthias CE Primary School, London

My Dream

As I am dreaming I am sailing through the sea
I can feel the cool breeze blowing in my face.
I can see the sea creatures swimming in the deep blue sea.
As the waves take me away.
My thoughts when I get back to shore are my feet touching the yellow crunching sand between my toes watching the seagulls flying above my head
Pecking at people's heads, also people's food.
I'm sitting in my deck chair with the hot sun burning my skin.

Shanique Titer (9)
St Matthias CE Primary School, London

The View!

I see an imaginary view that has now come true.
I am standing on a cliff where the shadows grew.
There's not a cloud today just a sky of blue.
As I reached for the stars I feel so new.
Although my heart was calling out for the stars,
My head knew it wasn't true.
I woke up in a sudden view of my room, as I knew the mysteries were no longer true.
I reached for the candles as I blew, wishing my dreams will now come true.

Mariya Ahmed (10)
St Matthias CE Primary School, London

Forest Creatures

I wake up in the morning sunrise
When I woke up I felt surprised
I feel like I am in danger
I know myself I am no stranger
Then I saw a fox talking; I gasped
'What are you doing here?' it asked
'I woke up here in the middle of the night.'
I complained.
'Did you know it actually rained?' it said.
'Wish I helped you instead.'
Then I woke up in my bed.

Ericka Kasongo (9)
St Matthias CE Primary School, London

Who's That Knocking At My Door?

Who's that knocking at my door?
I must admit I'm a little afraid.
Will it be a ghost or a dark black crow?
The wind whistled as I walked by.
In the gloomy dark place shadows crept around.
I'm scared, will it be a witch or a monster?
Someone opened the door as I walked closer and closer.
I saw a friendly ghost saying, 'Hello!'

Saffa Ahmed (10)
St Matthias CE Primary School, London

My Magical Mysterious Mirror

I look outside my window,
Seeing the foxes, squirrels and crows,
To me it seemed, like any other winter's day,
The sky still ominously tenebrous and grey.

I was told to come downstairs,
To see my clothes on the chairs,
So I tidied it up,
but the aroma of trouble held me up.

Then I caught it like a flu.

And so I told my parents so that they knew,
but then I saw a mirror,
looking at me like a reign of terror.

Luckily, I woke up in my bed,
Not daring to move because of all the dread.

Darren Kwo (11)
St Vincent De Paul RC Primary School, London

Imagine

Imagine all the things you can
So you can be a happy Dan.

Imagine if you were the
Child of a God whose story
was not yet told.
If you were to dream of that,
You wouldn't get old.

Imagine if you were a superhero,
rescuing dozens of people,
rescuing their families so they can be cheerful.

Imagine all the things you can
So you can be a happy Dan.
Imagine if you were a detective,
With skills like Scooby-Doo.
But with luck like that,
You'd encounter a ghost or two.

Imagine if you were a policeman
Rushing from crime to crime.
If you could do that, you'd have handcuffs that shine.

Imagine all the things you can,
So you can be a happy Dan.

Josh Herbie Pritchard (11)
St Vincent De Paul RC Primary School, London

Untitled

Dreams in your head they can escape,
they always come back to you like a wave.
The tingling of your feet when you're asleep that shows the excitement of your dreams.
Your friends, your family they're all smiling happily but then comes the man that makes it all a tragedy.
He stomped on the sand castle and breaks it all down; now the kids are crying all sat on the ground.
But Mum said, 'Don't have a frown!'
She gives out some lollies to share around the sea, the sand, it's all so fun,
but you wake up and it'll all be gone.

Giulia Caturano (10)
St Vincent De Paul RC Primary School, London

The Dinosaur That Played Football

When I was little I used to think,
'Could dinosaurs play football and score a hat-trick?'

When I think about it I feel like it's true,
I want to see them one day or two.

I look through the window
And what do I see,
a dinosaur looking right at me.
'Come here,' he said.
So I followed him to a football pitch.

He passed me the ball. I shot it top right.
I scored a great goal.
What a good night!

Fred Del Cerro (11)
St Vincent De Paul RC Primary School, London

In The Deep

I n the depth of the sea, seaweed dancing with the beat
N ever faulting the fish's swim. What beauty! Can you see?

T iny creatures crawl on the sea bed
H ermit crabs scurrying along
E normous school of fish.

D olphins diving through the crystal water
E asy gliding turtles swimming to the shore
E ndless crashing of waves on the rocks
P eacefully the water rolling up the sand.

Sally-Ann Forrest (10)
St Vincent De Paul RC Primary School, London

A Sunny Dream

In the future I'd like to be...

Under the shade of a green palm tree
With a monkey hanging around my neck
And the *tap, tap, tap, tap* of a woodpecker.

To be a zoologist is my dream
Under a bright sunny beam
With giraffes eating leaves
And monkeys swinging in the trees
I'll save a baby one
So we can have a lot of fun.

To be a zoologist is my dream
I'm good with animals it will seem!

Bianca Polloni (10)
St Vincent De Paul RC Primary School, London

That's Christmas Day!

C hristmas smell fills the air
H ollow wreaths everywhere
R eindeer galloping across the sky
I cy snowflakes twirling by
S tockings hung on the end of beds
T rees decorated gold and red
M ince pies, delicious and hot
A baby lying in a manger cot
S tars that guide the three kings all the way...

Jamie Eson-Benjamin (10)
St Vincent De Paul RC Primary School, London

Fake

F antasy can make you smile or weep
A lthough unicorns are great to fly on when you are asleep
K nowing that your fairy and dinosaur will never speak
E ternal happiness you make think until you wake up and blink!

Mia Moreschi (11)
St Vincent De Paul RC Primary School, London

Justice

J ustify the reason
U nderstanding the law
S upreme court decides
T rouble caused
I nterrogation time
C ease the criminal
E xpectations high.

Ruby Ella Carton (10)
St Vincent De Paul RC Primary School, London

Young**Writers**
Est.1991

YOUNG WRITERS INFORMATION

We hope you have enjoyed reading this book – and that you will continue to in the coming years.

If you're a young writer who enjoys reading and creative writing, or the parent of an enthusiastic poet or story writer, do visit our website **www.youngwriters.co.uk**. Here you will find free competitions, workshops and games, as well as recommended reads, a poetry glossary and our blog.

If you would like to order further copies of this book, or any of our other titles, then please give us a call or visit **www.youngwriters.co.uk**.

Young Writers
Remus House
Coltsfoot Drive
Peterborough
PE2 9BF
(01733) 890066
info@youngwriters.co.uk